THIS BOOK HAS BEEN DISCARDED
BY SKULL ISLAND PUBLIC LIBRARY

DINOSAURUSES
OF THE MOVIES
By John LeMay

Copyright © 2020 by Bicep Books.

All images reproduced within this book derive from memorabilia, publicity photos, and other publicity materials. This material appears here for the sole purpose of publicity and education. The publisher also wishes to acknowledge that they claim no rights to the underlying artistic works, photos, or images embodied in this book.

DINOSAURUSES
OF THE MOVIES

Carole Landis in One Million B.C. (1940).

Still from Gertie the Dinosaur *(1914), a short film in which a dinosaur does simple tricks for a showman.*

THE EARLY DAYS OF DINOSAURS ON FILM

The invention of the motion picture came about in the 1880s, long after the dinosaurs were dead. However, it didn't take the movies long to pick up on dinosaurs. In 1905 was produced an adaptation of a dinosaur comic called *Prehistoric Peeps*. Supposedly the dinosaurs were brought to life by men in costumes. We say supposedly because, sadly, *Prehistoric Peeps* is a lost film. Therefore, the earliest surviving dinosaur picture was the five minute cartoon, *Gertie the Dinosaur*, from 1914.

The same year as *Gertie the Dinosaur,* D.W. Griffith's *Brute Force* was released. Unlike *Gertie, Brute Force* was a live-action comedy short that begins in the modern-day. A man named Harry is upset that his girlfriend, Priscilla, has left a party with another man. "Oh, for the good old days of brute force and marriage by capture!" Harry's title card reads (as this film was made before the invention of sound in movies it was silent; therefore, the dialogue was printed onscreen). Harry then has a flashback to the good ol' days of prehistoric times. In the flashback, a caveman and his mate survive various perils, including something resembling a winged dragon more so than a dinosaur. Also popping up is a Ceratosaurus, animated via an art called stop-motion. Through this process, a special effects technician moves a dinosaur model one frame at a time. When all the frames are run together, it appears that the dinosaur is moving! As such, this was the first stop-motion dinosaur ever created.

Surviving image from **Brute Force** *(1914).*

The title character in The Dinosaur and the Missing Link *(1917).*

Next came *The Dinosaur and the Missing Link: A Prehistoric Tragedy*, a short film animated by Willis O'Brien in 1915. The movie was released later, in 1917, by Thomas Edison's film company Conquest Pictures. The comical story follows the efforts of a caveman trying to impress a cavegirl, with his attempts being thwarted by an ape, the missing link. The film is notable for being one of O'Brien's early works, and in 1933 he would do the special effects for the dinosaur extravaganza *King Kong*.

Still from The Ghost of Slumber Mountain *(1918).*

WILLIS O'BRIEN'S EARLY DINOSAUR MOVIES

The year after the release of *The Dinosaur and the Missing Link* Willis O'Brien made another dinosaur movie, *The Ghost of Slumber Mountain*. It was the first movie to mix stop-motion animation dinosaurs in with real actors. The tagline for the exciting film went, "These giant monsters of the past are seen to breathe, to live again, to move and battle as they did at the dawn of life!"

Today only about half of the real movie still exists. Originally, it ran 40 minutes long and contained 3,000 feet of film (or three reels)! Producers of the time felt it was too long and ordered the movie to be cut in half. Nobody knows what happened to the cut twenty minutes of footage.

The movie begins with an explorer named Jack Holmes (played by one of the producers, Herbert M. Dawley) telling his two nephews about a mysterious place called Slumber Mountain, near the "Valley of Dreams." There Jack finds a cabin that belonged to an old hermit, Mad Dick. The ghost of Mad Dick (Willis O'Brien) appears to Jack and tells him to use a magical telescope within the cabin to look out at Slumber Mountain. When he does, Jack sees a Brontosaurus, two Triceratops, and a Tyrannosaurus. The Tyrannosaurus sees Jack and begins to chase him. But, just before the beast reaches him, Jack wakes up. It was all a dream.

The T-Rex attacks a Triceratops in **Slumber Mountain.**

Next up was 1920's *Along the Moonbeam Trail*. Though this doesn't sound like the title of a dinosaur movie, it was. And it was just as fantastical as *The Ghost of Slumber Mountain*. In this story, a magical airplane transports two children to the Moon, where they observe various dinosaurs. Contrary to rumors that this movie merely recycled footage from *The Ghost of Slumber Mountain*, the dinosaur footage is all original. Furthermore, though Willis O'Brien is credited with this movie's effects, they were actually done by his former partner Herbert M. Dawley.

Image from Along the Moonbeam Trail *(1920).*

Scene from The Lost World *(1925)*.

THE LOST WORLD

In the year 1912, Sir Arthur Conan Doyle wrote his best known novel outside of his Sherlock Holmes series. That novel was *The Lost World*, which told of an expedition to a prehistoric plateau full of dinosaurs located in South America. By 1925, a film version had been produced. Though it wasn't the first movie to utilize stop-motion dinosaurs, it was the first widely successful one to do so. Because of its exposure, some people even thought that the dinosaurs were real!

The movie is fairly faithful to the book with a few differences, notably how it ends. But we'll get to that later. The movie opens with a girl named Paula White, who is distraught that her father has gone missing on an expedition in South America. She acquires the aid of Professor Challenger in London. Paula and Challenger also enlist the help of famed hunter Sir John Roxton, news reporter Edward Malone (who mostly wants to join the expedition to impress his fiancée), and others on their journey.

The expedition arrives on a plateau populated by dinosaurs and a villainous Apeman. Throughout the story, the characters endure numerous near death experiences at the hands of the Apeman and the claws of the dinosaurs. Eventually, it is discovered that Paula's father died on the plateau long ago. As the group makes preparations to leave, a volcanic eruption occurs, and they escape just in time.

Scene from 1925 adaptation of The Lost World.

At the base of the plateau, the expedition finds a brontosaurus stuck in the mud. They decide to bring it back to civilization with them, and this is where the movie and book differ, as no such thing happens in the novel. Overall, it's an exciting addition. The brontosaurus is brought to London but escapes its confines, terrorizing the city until it falls off the Tower Bridge and into the River Thames.

The film was a huge success and paved the way for more dinosaur movies to come. In 1931, *The Lost World* director Harry Hoyt planned a quasi-remake of the movie called *Creation*, with a similar story about an island of dinosaurs. The movie was eventually canceled by the producer, RKO Pictures, and replaced by another dinosaur movie: 1933's *King Kong*.

ONE MILLION B.C.

In 1940 came one of the better-known dinosaur movies, *One Million B.C.*, from producer Hal Roach. Unlike *The Lost World* and *King Kong*, it eschewed stop-motion effects in favor of men in suits and real animals disguised as dinosaurs.

The story begins with a modern-day prologue, where a group of hikers caught in a storm find shelter in a cave. Inside they meet an anthropologist who is studying cave paintings by ancient man on the cave wall. From the drawings, he tells them the story of a caveman named Tumak and we flash back to the stone age.

Tumak is a member of the Rock Tribe, a nasty bunch where only the strong survive. Tumak fights his father Akhoba over a piece of triceratops meat and falls from a cliff! Upon waking from his fall, Tumak is chased by a mammoth into a tree, which the mastodon knocks into a river. Tumak floats down the river until he is rescued by the beautiful Loana, a member of the Shell Tribe.

One of the "dinosaurs" in *One Million B.C.*

The stone age Romeo and Juliet story continues with Tumak trying to adjust to life in the more peaceful Shell Tribe. Tumak even proves his worth by fighting off an Allosaurus. But, later, Tumak fights another member of the tribe because Tumak wants the man's spear. Tumak is exiled, but Loana decides to go with him.

The two survive various dangers in the wilderness, including a giant prehistoric armadillo called a glyptodont. Eventually, the two become separated and Loana is kidnapped by the new, evil leader of the Rock Tribe. Tumak shows up to rescue her and defeats the man, and therefore becomes the new leader of the Rock Tribe.

Through Loana's influence, the Rock Tribe becomes more like the Shell Tribe. But then tragedy strikes. A volcano erupts, and many people are killed. Tumak and Loana are separated again. Tumak eventually finds Loana back with the Shell Tribe, under attack by a giant dinosaur. Everyone bands together to defeat the creature and a happy ending is had for all.

One Million B.C. would live on long after its 1940 release date due to effects footage from the film being used in nearly a dozen other movies like *Untamed Women* (1952), *Robot Monster* (1953), *The Lost Planet* (1953), *King Dinosaur* (1955), *Teenage Cave Man* (1958), and *Valley of the Dragons* (1961) to name only a few.

The Beast from 20,000 Fathoms *(1953)*.

MONSTER DINOSAURS

The 1950s saw the birth of a new trend in dinosaur movies: that of made-up dinosaur monsters. The first was the Rhedosaurus that appeared in *The Beast from 20,000 Fathoms* (1953). The whole movie was built around a short story called "The Fog Horn" by Ray Bradbury. In the story, a lonely surviving dinosaur hears the call of a foghorn and attacks a lighthouse. The movie version has a similar scene, but there's a lot more to it than a monster attacking a lighthouse. In the film, the dinosaur, which was awakened by atomic testing, attacks New York before it is killed. The effects were done by a man named Ray Harryhausen, who would go on to become just as well known as Willis O'Brien in the special effects world.

Next up was *Godzilla* (1954) from Japan, in which an irradiated dinosaur attacks Tokyo. Unlike stop-motion, *Godzilla* employed something called suitmation, in which a man in a rubber suit trampled miniature city sets. Godzilla was the first entry in an entire series that currently counts in at over a dozen movies!

Then came a quasi-remake of *The Beast from 20,000 Fathoms* called *The Giant Behemoth* in 1959. Actually, that movie didn't even start out with a dinosaur, and the monster, as envisioned by the writer, was an "amorphous blob of radiation." The movie's producers wanted to capitalize on the success of *The Beast from 20,000 Fathoms* and mandated that the monster become a dinosaur.

The Giant Behemoth *(1959).*

Still from Gorgo *(1961).*

Not coincidentally, the man who directed *Giant Behemoth* also directed *Beast from 20,000 Fathoms*. The director's name was Eugène Lourié, and he went on to make a third dinosaur monster movie in 1961. Unlike his previous two movies, made with stop-motion, this one used suitmation like *Godzilla* and was called *Gorgo*. As it turned out, Lourié's daughter had asked him to make a movie where the monster lived in the end, and so he did. *Gorgo* is about a group of salvage divers off the coast of Ireland who discover and capture the sea monster Gorgo. Unbeknownst to them, Gorgo is not fully grown and is just a baby! Gorgo is shipped off to a circus in London, while Gorgo's mother, Ogra, surfaces to destroy the fishing village where her baby was last seen in Ireland. Ogra comes to London to rescue her baby, and in the process destroys famous landmarks like the Big Ben clocktower. Though Ogra scuffles with the military, she rescues her baby. True to his word, Lourié's final shot is of the monsters swimming peacefully back to sea.

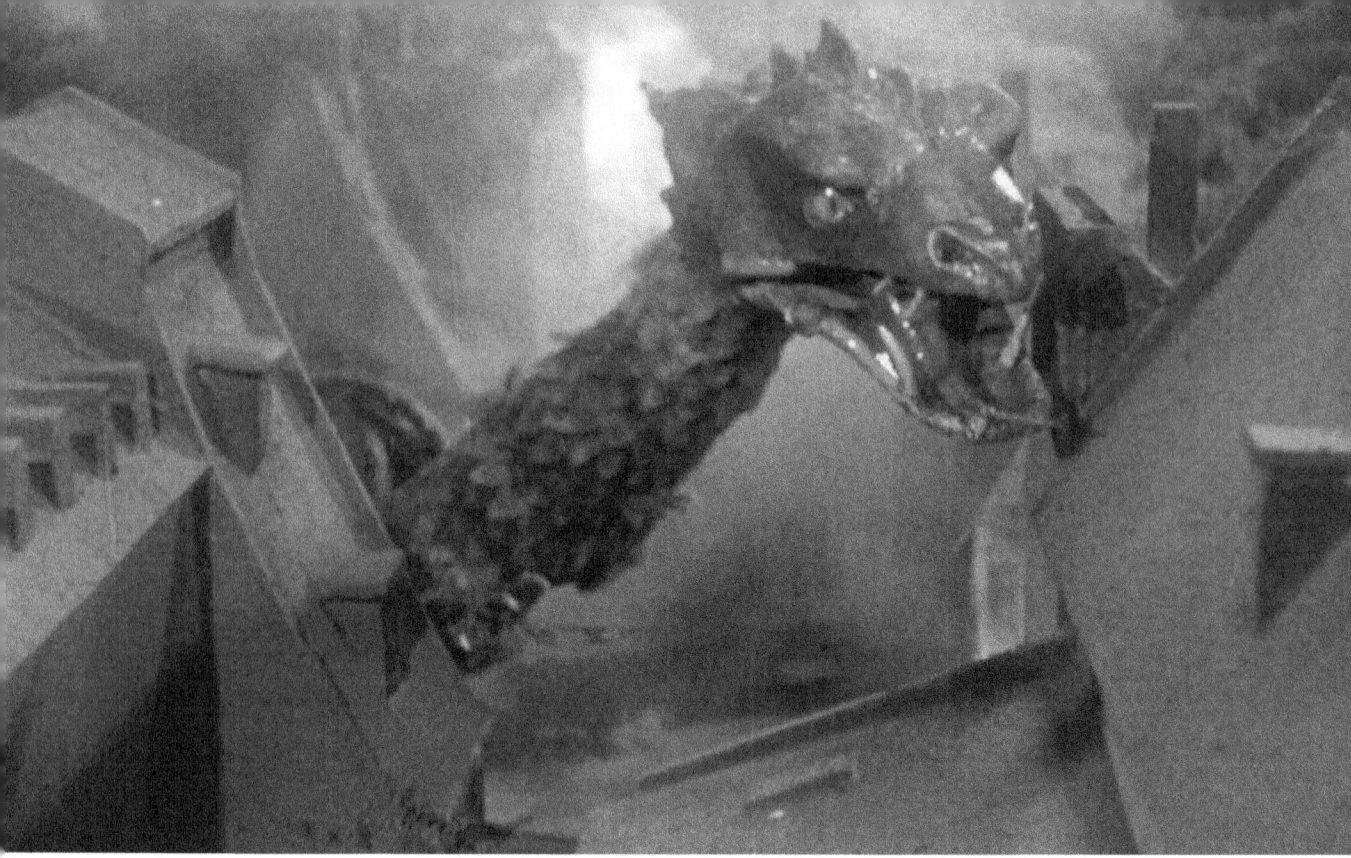

The title character in Reptilicus *(1961).*

That same year, another dinosaur monster came out of Europe: *Reptilicus*. The picture has an interesting origin in that it was partially inspired by a movie that didn't get made called *The Volcano Monsters*. Ib Melchoir wrote that movie in the late 1950s, and it reportedly would have had a Tyrannosaurus Rex and an Ankylosaurus revived from suspended animation. The two monsters would have then wrecked San Francisco as a scientist, his assistant, and a military man do their best to stop them. When that movie didn't get made, Melchoir simply took the characters and situations from that script and transplanted them into *Reptilicus*.

In *Reptilicus*, the severed tail of a prehistoric monster is found buried underground and is brought to Copenhagen for study. The tail then regenerates itself into a fully grown dinosaur monster called Reptilicus. However, Reptilicus wasn't based on any real dinosaur and looked more like a dragon. In the European version of the movie, Reptilicus even flew! But, the U.S. producers thought it looked silly and removed it. On the other hand, the U.S. producers gave Reptilicus its own power unique to the English speaking version: Reptilicus could now spit green slime!

Eventually, Reptilicus is finally rendered unconscious by a special sedative developed by the scientist characters, which is shot into its mouth from a bazooka fired by the military character. However, the movie ends with a shot of Reptilicus's severed foot resting on the ocean floor, just waiting to regenerate. Sequel anyone?

Rare still of the deleted flying scene from **Reptilicus**.

DINOSAURUS!

In addition to the monster dinosaurs that were Godzilla and Gorgo, traditional dinosaurs were still appearing in theaters too. 1960's *Dinosaurus* had frozen specimens of a Tyrannosaurus Rex and a Brontosaurus found underwater off the coast of a tropical island. The dead dinos are dredged ashore, but unbeknownst to all, they are really just in suspended animation. And that's not all, a caveman has also been recovered with them. Soon all three prehistoric survivors awaken and cause chaos all across the island.

Really, only the Tyrannosaurs is bad. The brontosaurus does little more than munch on plants, and the caveman befriends a young boy named Julio. The two even take a ride on the brontosaurus. Tragedy strikes when the Tyrannosaurus comes along and kills the good dinosaur, though. Then, the poor caveman dies saving Julio from an accident. The people of the island then band together to fight the Tyrannosaurus, and it is pushed off a cliff with a bulldozer.

RETURN TO THE PAST

The 1960s saw remakes of various dinosaur movies. First came a remake of *The Lost World* in 1960, starring Claude Rains and Jill St. John. The movie used giant lizards rather than stop-motion dinosaurs though and was a disappointment to many dinosaur fans.

In 1966, Hammer Films from England, famous for horror movies like *Horror of Dracula* and *Curse of Frankenstein*, tried their hand at dinosaurs with a remake of *One Million B.C.* Hammer called their version *One Million Years B.C.* and it was a big hit, prompting a sequel right away. However, due to the arduous nature of stop-motion animation, the sequel, *When Dinosaurs Ruled the Earth*, didn't come out until 1970.

The story in *When Dinosaurs Ruled the Earth* is the opposite of *One Million Years B.C.* Rather than an outcast caveman, it's an outcast cavewoman, Sana, who must journey across a prehistoric wasteland. Throughout her adventures, she becomes adopted by a giant dinosaur and falls in love with a member of the opposite tribe: Tara of the Shell People.

Sana is rescued at sea by Tara early in the film and the two form an instant bond. This doesn't sit well with Tara's girlfriend, who exiles Sana from the Shell Tribe. Not long after, Sana is attacked by a man-eating plant in the jungle, which chomps off some of her blonde hair. Tara finds the remains and assumes his lady love to be dead.

Victoria Vetri in When Dinosaurs Ruled the Earth *(1970).*

The Rhedosaurus inspired dino-star of When Dinosaurs Ruled the Earth.

Eventually, Sana takes cover in a recently hatched dinosaur egg. When the mother dinosaur (modeled after the Rhedosaurus) finds Sana in the egg the next morning, it thinks that Sana is her hatchling. For the rest of the movie, the dinosaur protects Sana from members of the Rock Tribe out to capture her.

When Sana can't be caught, the Rock Tribe kidnaps Tara instead and wishes to kill him. Sana sneaks into the camp and rescues him just as a massive typhoon occurs. The lovers survive the cataclysm while the evil cavemen all perish.

In Hammer's dinosaur movies, the cavewomen were just as much a draw as the dinosaurs were.

Though *When Dinosaurs Ruled the Earth* was a success, Hammer was disappointed with the amount of time it took to make. Therefore, for the next sequel, they dropped the dinosaurs altogether (had this not been the case, Hammer wanted to continue Sana's adventures in a sequel called *Dinosaur Girl*).

Toomak and Loana as they appear in Creatures That the World Forgot *(1971).*

In 1971, Hammer made *Creatures That the World Forgot*, which incidentally contains very few creatures! It repeats the story of *One Million Years B.C.* with two warring brothers, one of whom is again named Toomak. In place of the dinosaurs are a giant cave bear (just a man in a suit), a real live python, and a group of monstrous people called "the Mud Men."

EDGAR RICE BURROUGHS' DINOSAURS

Alongside Jules Verne, one of the more famous sci-fi writers of the early days was Edgar Rice Burroughs, the creator of Tarzan. In addition to the Ape Man, Burroughs also created the land of Caprona, a prehistoric island hidden behind walls of ice. On the island are dinosaurs, whole tribes of cavemen, and even winged humans! Burroughs wrote three books based around Caprona in this order: *The Land That Time Forgot*, *The People That Time Forgot*, and *Out of Time's Abyss*.

A dinosaur sneaks up on one of the cast of Land That Time Forgot *(1974).*

Doug McClue in Land That Time Forgot *(1974).*

In 1974, Amicus Productions in England took it upon themselves to adapt *The Land That Time Forgot*. Rather than stop-motion, small dinosaur puppets were used to bring the beasts to life. There were also life-sized props created of a plesiosaur head and a full-scale pterodactyl.

The movie is faithful to the book, and begins during World War I. A Brittish ship is sunk by a German U-Boat, which picks up the survivors lead by Bowen Tyler (Doug McClure). The combined Brittish and American survivors overtake the submarine, but it drifts off course until it reaches the frozen island of Caprona. The U-Boat

takes an underwater passage into the island, docking in a prehistoric lagoon. The Germans and the Brittish/American camp form a truce to repair the submarine and leave the island, which is crawling with cavemen and dinosaurs.

The movie ends with a villainous German officer commandeering the submarine and leaving Bowen and his girlfriend, Lisa, behind as Caprona is consumed by a volcanic eruption. Ironically, Bowen and Lisa survive while the submarine explodes. The movie was a big hit with children, ensuring a sequel.

Some of the decidedly non-dinosaurian monsters of At the Earth's Core *(1976).*

Before returning to Caprona, Amicus decided to take a detour to *At the Earth's Core* in 1976, based on another Edgar Rice Burroughs novel of the same name. Doug McClure returned in the lead role, this time as David Innes. He was joined by famous horror star Peter Cushing as Dr. Abner Perry. The duo travel to the titular destination by way of the Iron Mole, a huge boring machine that drills deep into the earth. At the earth's core, David and Perry find a race of caveman-like peoples subjugated by a race of psychic pterodactyls called the Mahars. There are a few other gigantic dinosaur-like creatures, such as a four-legged, dog-like reptile that Innes must combat. But, otherwise, *At the Earth's Core* was light on dinosaurs and most of the underground creatures seemed to be made up (such as a fire breathing frog!).

Amicus and McClure returned to Caprona for *The People That Time Forgot* (1977), in which Major Ben McBride (Patrick Wayne, son of John Wayne) leads a rescue mission to find Tyler. He arrives via aeroplane, which is brought down by a pterodactyl. McBride and his cohorts must trek across Caprona on foot. In the process they befriend a cavewoman named Ajor, who informs them that Tyler was captured by an evil race called the Naga.

In truth, the Naga are a scaled-down version of the winged men, called the Weiroo, who appear in *Out of Time's Abyss*, not *The People That Time Forgot* novel. *Out of Time's Abyss* ended with McBride and Tyler departing Caprona on the German U-Boat. You see, *The Land That Time Forgot* novel never ended with the U-Boat exploding like the movie did. While the book trilogy has a happy ending, *The People That Time Forgot* movie sadly does not. Tyler is rescued from the Naga, but dies while escaping. McBride and his cohorts then make it back to the plane as Caprona begins to erupt.

Doug McClure and Dana Gillespie in **People** That Time Forgot.

Some of the dinosaurs from People That Time Forgot *(1977).*

DINOSAUR MOVIES TODAY

The same year that *People That Time Forgot* was released, so was *Star Wars*. Modern blockbusters like *Jaws* and *Star Wars* had an interesting effect on dinosaur movies in the year 1977 as *Star Wars* seemingly inspired the outer-space based movie *Planet of Dinosaurs*, while *Jaws* inspired a dinosaur movie from Japan.

Planet of Dinosaurs opens with an exciting spaceship crash onto an alien planet. An escape capsule crashes into a lake, so the crew must swim to shore. Within moments, one of them is eaten by a prehistoric monster that lives in the water!

As the space-aged survivors continue to trek across the planet, they discover it is overrun with prehistoric monsters. In their travels to find a safe place to live, they come across a brontosaurus, stegosaurus, styracosaurus, tyrannosaurus, and even a giant spider. The Tyrannosaurus ends up being the most challenging adversary of them all and eats several of the crew until only five survivors remain. The crew then lures the T-Rex into a trap, causing it to run and impale itself onto a huge stake in the ground, killing it for good. The survivors then decide to make a new life for themselves on the prehistoric planet, no longer concerned with being rescued.

Two of the titular titans of **Planet of Dinosaurs.**

Still from Toei's Legend of Dinosaurs and Monster Birds *(1977).*

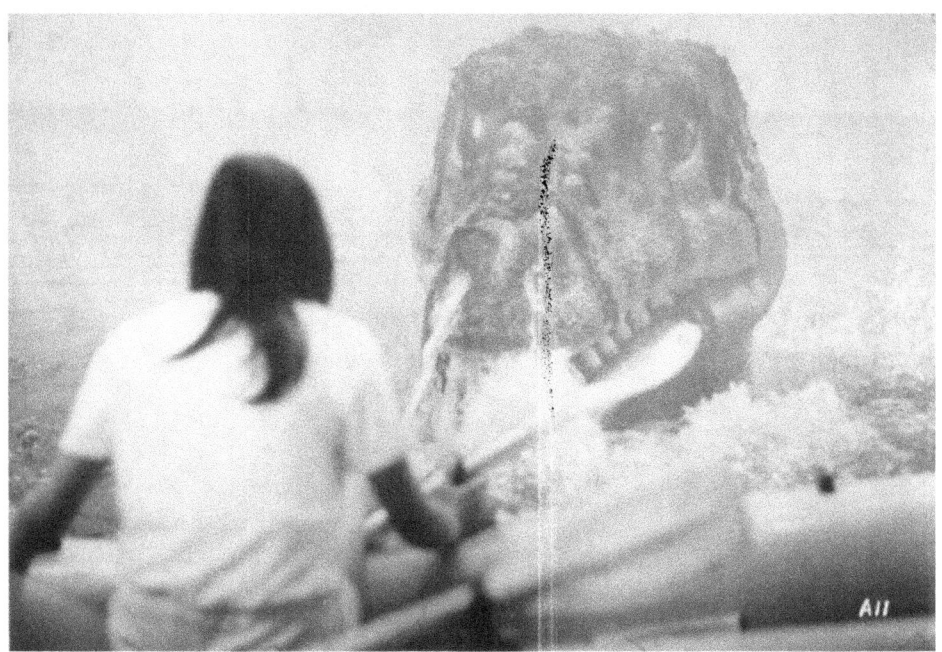
The plesiosaur surfaces to terrorize another victim.

Over in Japan, Toei studios was influenced by *Jaws* to produce *The Legend of Dinosaurs and Monster Birds.* The spooky story begins with a woman discovering an ice cave full of giant eggs in a forest near Mt. Fuji. As the woman peers into one of the cracked eggs, a monstrous eye stares back at her, and she runs from the cave screaming. Her story reaches a geologist named Ashizawa who travels to a Mt. Fuji lake where stories abound of dinosaurs and dinosaur eggs. In the waters of Lake Sai is a live plesiosaurus that eats several people.

After the death of a woman visiting the lake on a scuba diving trip, Lake Sai becomes the sight of an all-out media frenzy. The dinosaur hunt turns up nothing, but as the movie progresses, one of the eggs hatches and a giant Rhamphorynchus pops out. We call it giant because in real life, a Rhamphorynchus was not a very large dino-

Ashizawa and Akiko encounter the plesiosaurus.

saur. In fact, technically, the plesiosaurus and Rhamphorynchus were prehistoric reptiles, but not actual dinosaurs.

At the same time that the flying dinosaur is terrorizing a local village, Ashizawa and a female scuba diver, Akiko, have braved the lake's depths to search for the plesiosaur. The duo eventually surfaces in what was once the ice cave from the beginning of the movie, only now its melting and one of the eggs has hatched.

Ashizawa and Akiko walk into the forest of Mt. Fuji to find the plesiosaur roaming around. Soon, the Rhamphorynchus shows up to battle the other prehistoric giant. The battle is so intense that Mt. Fuji erupts, consuming both dinosaurs in rivers of lava.

To bring the dinosaurs to life full-sized props of the head, neck, tail, and fins of the plesiosaur were created. However, in the Godzilla tradition, a few shots of the plesiosaur from the climax actually utilized a man in a suit!

But, sadly, neither *Legend of Dinosaurs and Monster Birds* nor *Planet of Dinosaurs* were big hits when released, leaving the future of dinosaur movies uncertain.

But, even though the landscape of special effects movies continues to change, hopefully movie dinosaurs aren't in danger of going extinct anytime soon…

Still from **Planet of Dinosaurs** *(1977).*

THE BIG BOOK OF JAPANESE GIANT MONSTER MOVIES SERIES

VOLUME 1: 1954-1982

VOLUME 2: 1984-2017

THE LOST FILMS

TERROR OF THE LOST TOKUSATSU FILMS

WRITING JAPANESE MONSTERS

EDITING JAPANESE MONSTERS

KONG UNMADE: THE LOST FILMS OF SKULL ISLAND

Be sure to read these other great books!

www.ingramcontent.com/pod-product-compliance
Lightning Source LLC
Chambersburg PA
CBHW081237080526
44587CB00022B/3972